Third Edition

$11

In OUR
Own Words

Student Writers at Work

TEACHER'S MANUAL

REBECCA MLYNARCZYK
Kingsborough Community College
City University of New York

STEVEN B. HABER
New Jersey City University

CAMBRIDGE
UNIVERSITY PRESS

CAMBRIDGE UNIVERSITY PRESS
Cambridge, New York, Melbourne, Madrid, Cape Town, Singapore, São Paulo, Delhi

Cambridge University Press
32 Avenue of the Americas, New York, NY 10013-2473, USA

www.cambridge.org
Information on this title: www.cambridge.org/9780521540292

First published 2005
2nd printing 2008

Printed in the United States of America

A catalog record for this book is available from the British Library

ISBN-13 978-0-521-54028-5 student's book
ISBN-10 0-521-54028-3 student's book
ISBN-13 978-0-521-54029-2 teacher's book
ISBN-10 0-521-54029-1 teacher's book

Cambridge University Press has no responsibility for
the persistence or accuracy of URLs for external or
third-party Internet Web sites referred to in this book,
and does not guarantee that any content on such
Web sites is, or will remain, accurate or appropriate.

Book design and layout services: Page Designs International

CONTENTS

INTRODUCTION

The title of this book, *In Our Own Words: Student Writers at Work*, emphasizes our belief that students write best when they are free to write about subjects that engage them in a voice that is their own. The idea for the book originated with the discovery that ESL and bilingual college students respond positively to writing by other student writers. That is why 85 percent of the readings in the Student's Book are by student writers rather than by professional journalists. The student essays are not intended as models but rather as a stimulus for discussion, inspiration, and further writing. The enthusiastic reactions from students and teachers who have used the first two editions have confirmed our belief in the value of highlighting student writing in the classroom.

Through this text, students share the experiences of living or having lived in two cultures, the difficulties of learning a new language, and the challenges of overcoming obstacles in the pursuit of an education. There is also the shared experience of encountering an academic setting. Many students are the first in their families to attend college. For those who find being in an academic setting unfamiliar, uncomfortable, or threatening, the presentation of student writing sends a clear message: You are welcome here; your writing is welcome here.

We realize, however, that no matter how welcoming the environment, good writing does not just happen. Carefully designed activities, suggestions, and assignments provide the structure that enables developing writers to explore their own thoughts and find their own words. Throughout this Teacher's Manual, we have included teaching tips based on our classroom experiences. These tips will be helpful in creating an interactive writing class. We hope that the third edition of *In Our Own Words* will continue to inspire new writers and new writing.

GUIDING PRINCIPLES

In Our Own Words motivates students to take themselves seriously as writers and actively engage in writing as a communicative process. The book accomplishes these goals by:

- Engaging students' interest through reading selections by other students on high-interest themes
- Increasing students' motivation to write
- Including classroom activities that encourage students to see writing as a social process
- Encouraging students to reflect on their own writing

STRUCTURE OF THE STUDENT'S BOOK

Part I: Starting Out

Part I establishes the foundation for the rest of the book as students experience writing as a social process involving genuine communication.

In Chapter 1, students are encouraged to form a classroom community in which they can think and write about their attitudes toward and past experiences with writing. They can explore strategies for writing without worrying and consider ways of coping with common writing problems, such as choosing an appropriate topic or overcoming writer's block.

Part II: Personal Writing

In Part II, students write about topics of interest from their own experience.

In Chapters 2, 3, and 4, students write personal essays about experiences, people, and places that have influenced them deeply. These chapters encourage students to describe vividly but also to analyze how their lives have been shaped by the experiences, people, and places they are writing about.

Part III: More Formal Writing

In Part III, students practice more formal writing as they begin to analyze their own experiences and attitudes in the light of larger societal forces.

Chapter 5 serves as a transitional chapter in which students use interviews they have conducted as the basis for an analytic essay. They may choose between interviewing someone and writing about a theme in that person's life or interviewing one or more individuals for information on a topic of interest that will be the focus of their essay. In this chapter, students are introduced to the traditional academic practice of formulating a thesis statement.

In Chapter 6, students write a traditional reading-based essay using one or more print sources from the chapter. The topic is one familiar to every college student: how families are changing in the modern world. Not only do students comment on their print sources, they must also summarize and paraphrase ideas from these sources.

In Chapter 7, students write a brief research paper that includes identification of their sources according to APA or MLA style. As in the previous chapters, the topics are of high interest: (1) the influence of such factors as race, ethnicity, and immigration status on the formation of personal identity, and (2) an assessment of the possible advantages and disadvantages of interracial marriage. Students are required to use at least three research sources, one of which must be a reading in the chapter, another from the Internet, and a third that includes statistical information. They are encouraged to consider articles, books, and journals for their sources as well as personally conducted interviews.

CHAPTER ORGANIZATION OF THE STUDENT'S BOOK

In each chapter of Parts II and III, students do the following:

- Read and respond to some or all of the **Readings** at the beginning of the chapter
- Practice one or more of the **Techniques Writers Use**, which facilitate the type of writing called for in the chapter
- Do an **Internet Search** designed to generate ideas for writing or provide background information
- Draft an **Essay** on the general theme of the chapter
- Discuss the draft with a partner or group using the **Peer Response Form** at the end of the chapter
- Reflect on their own writing processes and on the feedback they have received (A **Writer's Plan for Revising** form is included at the end of each chapter in Part III.)
- **Revise** the essay in light of the feedback received
- Focus on correctness by doing the **Grammar in Context** tasks, which call attention to grammatical structures and encourage experimentation with language forms
- **Edit** the essay, paying special attention to the grammar point emphasized in the chapter
- **Proofread** the essay and make needed corrections

Three opportunities for student self-assessment are provided:

> **Goals for This Course:** *A Beginning Survey* (at the end of Chapter 1, page 24)
>
> **Assessing Your Progress:** *A Midterm Survey* (at the end of Chapter 4, page 122)
>
> **Assessing Your Progress:** *A Closing Survey* (at the end of Chapter 7, page 254)

The *Answer Key* for the grammar activities is provided at the end of the Student's Book so that students can work independently to correct their own work.

In Our Own Words contains a wealth of activities. We hope that teachers and students will feel free to move back and forth among the different sections of the book, using those parts that suit their own interests and needs.

PART I
STARTING OUT

Part I establishes the foundation for the rest of the book as students experience writing as a social process involving genuine communication. The activities in Part 1 are designed to be used at the beginning of a course; however, they can also be used in conjunction with later chapters.

Thinking of Yourself as a Writer

Chapter 1

In this chapter, students are encouraged to form a classroom community in which they can think and write about their attitudes toward and past experiences with writing. They can explore strategies for writing without worrying and consider ways of coping with common writing problems, such as choosing an appropriate topic or overcoming writer's block.

FORMING A CLASSROOM COMMUNITY (pages 4–7)

The purpose of this section is to create an environment that is conducive to transforming the writing experience from a display of competence to an act of communication. Students are encouraged to explore ideas freely and to share them with peers and with the teacher. While some students may welcome this workshop atmosphere, others may take some time to get used to it or even resist it. Speak privately with such students in order to explain the rationale for the activities.

Getting Acquainted (page 4)

Before beginning this activity, tell students that they are going to do some research about their classmates. They will be asked to report the results of their findings, and so it is important that they take notes. Direct the students to the survey on pages 4 and 5 and tell them they will have 10 minutes to complete it. Once the surveys are complete, give the students another 10 to 15 minutes to write up their results following the instructions on page 5. The results can then be handed in or discussed in class.

Looking at Similarities and Differences (page 5)

Give students about 10 minutes to interview each other using the questions on pages 5 and 6. At the conclusion of the interview, students classify the types of information they found into three categories: organization, creativity, or independence. Next they develop at least two generalizations about their partner as compared to themselves. Students then discuss their generalizations with the partner they interviewed. This can lead to a more extended writing assignment in which the student writes a comparison-contrast essay using the information from the survey as supporting details for generalizations.

Silent Conversations (page 7)

The purpose of this activity is to demonstrate the value of writing as a means of personal communication. Divide students into pairs and tell them to identify a topic for conversation that interests both students in the pair. Give the students a few minutes to talk about their topics. After the time is up, tell the students to stop talking and to continue their conversation in writing. After they have finished writing and reading each other's comments, they can discuss the differences between communicating in speech as opposed to communicating in writing using the bulleted questions in number 5 on page 7.

THINKING ABOUT WRITING (pages 8–11)

In this section, students assess their own attitudes and approaches toward writing and then compare their experience to that of other students.

Attitudes Toward Writing (page 8)

The purpose of this activity is to help students assess their own attitudes toward writing and to identify common negative attitudes that may stand in the way of writing progress. By comparing their own attitudes with those of others, students realize that they are not alone in their ambivalence toward writing. After students write about their attitudes, lead a class discussion, allowing them to verbalize whatever feelings they have about writing. Then ask the class to try to come up with ways of overcoming negative attitudes.

Past Experiences with Writing (page 9)

Give students time to read the sample questions and answers regarding past experiences with writing on pages 9–10. These can then be discussed either in small groups or as a whole class. Give students 10 to 15 minutes to write about their own past experiences with writing, following the guidelines given in step 2 on page 11. The small group discussion at the end is designed to help students realize that the difficulties they face with writing are not unique and that their classmates are a potential support group in overcoming writing problems.

WRITING WITHOUT WORRYING (pages 11–15)

The activities in this section are designed to help students warm up or get started on writing projects. Wherever possible, try out the activities before assigning them to students because this will help with understanding the challenges of the activity and with anticipating any problems the students may experience.

Modeling all new activities as they are introduced in the classroom is strongly recommended. Models can be introduced in a number of ways. For example, to model freewriting, do a brief freewriting on the blackboard or overhead projector in front of the class. A freewriting sample, either by the teacher or by a student, can be typed up and copied for the class to read and discuss. One such model is provided in step 1 on page 12. The purpose of modeling is to give the students a general idea of the appropriate type of writing for the activity. The models also stimulate ideas and help students get started with their own writing.

Freewriting (page 12)

Before students are introduced to the freewriting activity, it is useful to discuss with the class who the audience for their freewriting will be. Usually freewriting is not intended to be shared with others; if it will be shared, students should be told in advance. Writers use freewriting to brainstorm, keep track of their ideas, or in some cases to simply overcome frustration or anxiety about the writing process itself. Before asking the students to freewrite, tell them that their writing will not be collected and that they will not be required to share it with anyone unless they choose to do so. It is important for students to realize that freewriting is most effective if it is done quickly and without stopping. Some students may not feel comfortable writing without stopping to correct errors or look up words in the dictionary. These students might be reminded that this is only an experiment and to try their best to follow the guidelines on page 12.

Once students have done some freewriting, give them the opportunity to talk about the freewriting process either in small groups or as a class. Some students may wish to read their freewriting aloud at this point, but this should be on a voluntary basis. It is important to recognize that this technique works better for some students than others. This is why we introduce a variety of writing activities: so students can discover which works best for them.

Some teachers like to use freewriting on a recurring basis as a means of prewriting or brainstorming for a specific topic. This can be done by simply writing a prompt on the blackboard – for example, a word related to the topic – and then asking students to freewrite for five to ten minutes before beginning a reading or discussion on the topic.

Keeping a Journal (page 13)

As with freewriting, it is important for students to see the journal as a place where they can feel free to brainstorm, take notes, and develop ideas freely. If possible, provide an excerpt from a journal entry of your own so that students can see a sample entry in addition to the sample in step 1 on page 13. Then give students 10 to 15 minutes to write their own journal entries on one of the given topics.

One approach is to allocate a few minutes of class time per session for journal writing. Another is to assign it for homework and collect it periodically, writing comments to the student on his or her journal entries. It is important that if the journal will be collected by the teacher or shared with other students, the teacher let the class know this in advance. It is also important that in their responses neither teachers nor other students criticize grammar, but respond to the ideas expressed. In cases where a student's ideas are unclear, simply write a question or ask the student in conference what he or she had intended to say. Sharing their journals with a teacher, a partner, or a small group is an excellent way for students to write for an audience without worrying about grammatical correctness. Thus, the journals become avenues for ongoing communication.

There are many types of journals, and teachers should choose to assign the type that best suits the needs of the class. These are three of the most common types:

- A *freewriting journal* is unrestricted in content and provides students with a safe place to experiment, to explore new ideas, and to discuss their private thoughts.
- Another type of journal is a *reading journal*, in which students are asked to write brief summaries and reactions to the readings they are doing for the course. These journals provide opportunities to reflect upon and analyze the readings. The journals also allow the teacher to engage the student in a personal dialogue about the text.
- A third type of journal is a *topic journal*, in which students record information and thoughts about current issues such as social problems, politics, and technology. Entries can be drawn from the news media, personal conversations, class discussions, or any other source. As students actively search for material for this type of journal, they develop an awareness of issues to which they might otherwise pay little attention. These journals may also be used as the basis for small group or class discussions about topical issues.

If students make regular journal entries throughout the course, the journals become a place to develop ideas for writing projects, a place to plan future writing projects, and a place to reflect on work already done.

An important factor in deciding whether or not to collect students' journals is how much time the teacher has available to comment on this writing. We admit that the prospect of reading and commenting on thirty, forty, or more journals on top of everything else teachers are supposed to do may not be appealing. However, if the journal is to fulfill its role as a means of communication, it is important that it be responded to in some way. The purposes of the journals and methods of responding will determine how often they are collected. It could be as often as once a week or as infrequently as three or four times a semester.

The following suggestions may make the job of responding easier:

- Avoid making grammar and spelling corrections in the journals. In most writing courses, there should be ample opportunities for this type of editing work outside of the journals. If students ask why their journals are not being corrected, consider saying, "The purpose of the journal is to communicate and explore your own ideas. Right now, I am more interested in what you have to say than in how you say it. Later on, when we write more formal essays, we will work on the grammar, spelling, and punctuation."

- Lengthy comments in student journals are not necessary. Sometimes a simple check mark in the margin to signify something you liked can be enough. At other times, a few words of encouragement may mean more than a detailed commentary. Try to be specific about what you liked. If you disagree with an opinion expressed in the journal, perhaps pose a question such as, "Is it true that all women want to stay home and take care of children?" The important thing is that the student knows you have read the journal and have thought about it.

- Match up students with a journal partner. Once or twice a week during class, students can exchange journals and write responses to their partner's recent entries. From time to time, teachers can collect the journals and partner responses.

- An increasing number of teachers are relying on online journals in which students make their entries either via e-mail or on Weblogs, or "blogs." The teacher and other members of the class may respond to a student's journal entry electronically. These types of journals are easy to access and share and can be responded to more quickly and with more extended dialogues than are possible in the traditional notebook journal.

Interactive Writing (page 14)

As with freewriting or journal writing, the emphasis here is on communication, although there should be a little more attention to form and spelling. Students can do this activity in class following the guidelines on page 14, or they can do this as an e-mail assignment out of class, possibly sending a copy to the teacher throughout the correspondence. The teacher should specify the number of exchanges students are expected to complete in a given time frame.

Writing Without a Dictionary (page 15)

This activity is designed to make students aware of the advantages of foregoing the use of a dictionary, at least during the drafting stages of the writing process. The reason for this is to encourage students to get their ideas down on paper in a rough draft before making corrections during the revising and editing stages of the writing process. In addition, as an increasing number of students are now writing their first drafts using word processing programs with built-in spell-checkers, the dictionary is becoming less important during the drafting stage.

COPING WITH WRITING PROBLEMS (pages 15–22)

This section is designed to help students deal with a variety of writing challenges. The activities do not have to be done in any particular order nor do they all need to be done at the outset of the course. For example, the activities in *Choosing a Topic, Adjusting to Different Purposes and Audiences,* and *Dealing with Writer's Block* might be done near the beginning of the course, but the activity for *Doing Well on College Papers* could wait until the students move into more academic writing later on.

Choosing a Topic (page 16)

In most classes, it is the teacher who chooses the topic for writing. There are many practical reasons to justify this practice, such as focusing the topic in a manageable way or coordinating class work so that all students are working on the same thing at the same time.

However, there are some advantages to letting students choose their own topics some of the time. First, it places the responsibility for the assignment on the students rather than on the teacher. This may help them to trust their own judgment and to anticipate the interests of an audience. Second, when students are free to choose their topics, teachers have an opportunity to learn what is interesting or important to their students.

If students have never chosen their own writing topics before, this may at first be a somewhat bewildering experience. That is why it is important to model the process by which writers narrow down their own fields of possible topics. Do this by listing four or five writing topics on the blackboard – that is, topics you might choose to write about if you suddenly found yourself in a class with such an assignment. Then discuss your possible choices with the students, not so that they will choose these same topics, but so that they can see what kinds of issues are involved when making the decision. For example, a teacher's list might look like this:

> My new haircut
> My grandfather's 95th birthday
> The problems with cell phones
> The man who sleeps in my doorway

The teacher could then discuss his or her own thoughts about these topics, why he or she chose them, and which one would be most promising as a writing topic. After modeling the process, students can then begin to choose their own topics, following the steps on pages 16–17.

Adjusting to Different Purposes and Audiences (page 17)

This activity is designed to sensitize students to the need to adjust the form, content, and style of writing according to the purpose and audience for the writing. In this case, the students will write three short pieces – each with a different purpose and audience – as instructed on page 17.

Dealing with Writer's Block (page 18)

The purpose of this activity is to make students aware that the phenomenon known as writer's block commonly afflicts both professional and student writers and that there are effective solutions available. After reading the statements from various writers, have students write about their own experiences with writer's block, as instructed in step 2 on page 19. As students report the results of their discussions to the class (steps 3 and 4), record on the blackboard any strategies that students have used to overcome writer's block. Numerous articles suggesting strategies for dealing with writer's block can be found on the Internet by typing the keywords *overcoming writer's block* into any major search engine. Students can be assigned to read through some of these Web sites and come to class with a list of strategies they found.

Doing Well on College Papers (page 20)

The purpose of this activity is to help students identify strategies for writing successful college papers by surveying other students at their colleges or universities. The activity begins with students reading and discussing the four sample interviews with student writers. Students then conduct interviews outside of the classroom to find out how other students have dealt with the challenges of academic writing. The activity concludes with students sharing what they have learned. Write the strategies discussed on the blackboard for students to record in their notebooks.

In addition to having students conduct interviews, you may want to have them explore some of the many Web sites sponsored by college writing centers. These sites contain a wealth of useful suggestions and resources for student writers. Such sites can be found by entering the keywords *student resources writing* or *writing center* into any major search engine. (See A Word of Caution About the Internet on page 28 of this manual.)

A NOTE BEFORE YOU CONTINUE (page 23)

At this point, students should complete the *Goals for This Course: A Beginning Survey* on page 24, in which they are asked to outline their writing goals for the course. It is important that students understand the value of setting reasonable goals and take responsibility for fulfilling them. (Note that a midterm self-assessment is provided on page 122, and a final self-assessment is on page 254.)

A *Beginning Survey* is designed to help students identify their strengths as writers and also the areas in which they wish to improve. Additionally, the survey helps students identify strategies and resources that will help them develop as writers. This survey will be most effective if it is completed early in the course, typically no later than the end of the third week of classes. It is useful to return to the goals at the midterm and again in the final week, preferably during student-teacher conferences, so that students can see for themselves how much progress they have made toward their goals and revise or fine-tune their goals as necessary.

A student-teacher conference is an ideal way to discuss students' surveys, to understand how they perceive themselves as writers, and to provide individual guidance.

Tips on Student-Teacher Conferences

Student-teacher conferences can be used for many purposes in addition to discussing students' progress and goals. A conference can be a simple two- or three-minute discussion about the student's choice of topic, or it can be a more extended analysis as to how a thesis can be developed with supporting examples. The following are some suggestions for different types of conferences that can occur at various stages during a writing course.

- *Prewriting*
  Discuss the assignment. What is required? What will the topic be? Can it be narrowed down? How long should the essay be? Does the student have any personal experience or knowledge that can be included in the essay? Is research required, and if so, what sources will be used? Will an outline or diagram be helpful to organize ideas before writing? What would be a good topic sentence to introduce this essay?

- *Drafting*
  It is sometimes useful to simply sit and observe a student as he or she is drafting an essay on a computer. The teacher observes the student's choice of words, development of a topic sentence, use of examples, or even how the student uses the spell-checker. The teacher can then give the student feedback on his or her writing process, pointing out what seems to be working well and what might be changed. In another type of drafting conference, the teacher can ask the student to pause after having completed a topic sentence or paragraph and to discuss what has been written so far and what the student plans to write next.

- *Revising*

  Once the student has completed a draft, he or she should assess the
  work by answering the questions on the *Peer Response Forms* that appear
  throughout the book. There are also a number of excellent rubrics available
  online, which can be found by entering the keywords *writing rubrics* in any
  major search engine. Once the student has assessed his or her own draft,
  the teacher can comment. In a conference about revising, the points of
  emphasis are ideas, development, examples, and organization. Discussion
  of grammar, spelling, and punctuation – where they do not interfere with
  the clarity of ideas – can be postponed until the editing stage. Some
  teachers require several rounds of revising before the submission of a final
  draft.

- *Editing*

  After the student has completed the requisite number of revisions, it is
  time to focus on grammar, spelling, punctuation, and mechanics. As with
  revising, it is best to begin by asking the students if they can find any
  errors themselves. When pointing out student errors, rather than making
  corrections for the student, the teacher can simply point to an error and
  ask, "What's wrong here?" If the student still cannot make the correction,
  the teacher can provide some hints or state the rule if one applies.

- *Portfolio*

  Many writing courses now include portfolio assessment, in which students
  are asked to submit a selection of essays representative of their writing
  abilities. For this type of conference, the goal is to help the student identify
  his or her own writing strengths and weaknesses. Portfolios are often
  accompanied by a rubric designed to help students assess their own work.
  In some cases students and teachers use the same rubric to assess the
  portfolio independently. They then compare their respective assessments
  during the conference.

- *Progress and goals*

  Conferences devoted to identifying student goals for the course and
  assessing progress toward those goals can be a valuable part of the
  assessment process. The three self-assessment surveys provided in the
  Student's Book can be the basis for such conferences.

PART II
PERSONAL WRITING

In Part II, students write about topics of interest from their own experiences.

In Chapters 2, 3, and 4, students write personal essays about experiences, people, and places that have influenced them deeply. These essays involve students in writing vivid descriptions but also in analyzing how their lives have been shaped by the experiences, people, and places they are writing about.

Chapter 2 Experiences

READINGS (pages 30–44)

The six student essays in this chapter are presented to encourage students to reach back into their memories and to write about personal experiences.

Reading 1 (page 30)

Learning How to Cook *Florence Cheung*

This student essay demonstrates that an ordinary childhood experience can become an interesting subject for writing. The many details included show rather than tell why the experience was so memorable to the writer.

Before students read, ask them to think about the questions that appear at the beginning of the essay. These questions not only assist in preparing for the content of the essay but also may be used to generate topics for future writing. In most of the *Reflecting on the Reading* sections, there will be at least one question (usually question 4) that asks students to write a response based on these questions.

Reflecting on the Reading (page 31)

The reflection questions for this reading as well as those for all the readings in the book can be answered individually, by partners, in small groups, or as part of a whole-class discussion. Regardless of the method used, it is generally a good idea to allow students time to write their responses individually prior to reporting their answers to the group or to the whole class. A period of written reflection provides not only additional writing practice but also offers the student time to formulate a thoughtful answer. This is especially useful for students who are shy or hesitant to speak during class discussions.

For question 4, ask the students to consider the following questions: *When and where did it take place? How old were you at the time? Who else was present? What were the steps involved? What was the outcome? How did you feel about the experience?* Another way of doing the freewriting is to read each question aloud and then pause a minute or two between each one in order to allow students to write their answers quickly.

Reading 2 (page 32)

What Is It Like to Have an Empty Stomach? *Youssef Rami*

Before students read, ask them to think about the prereading questions.

Reflecting on the Reading (page 33)

Question 2 on page 33 asks students to analyze the use of direct versus indirect quotations in the essay. This is important because students frequently want to use both direct and indirect quotes in their narratives. The activity emphasizes awareness of the proper conventions and grammar to use in these situations.

Reading 3 (page 34)

A Teacher for a Day *Luisa Tiburcio*

Prior to reading, ask students to freewrite on the words *fear* and *excitement*. Write parts of some students' freewriting on the board. After the reading, return to these samples from the freewriting and ask students to identify connections to them in the text.

Reflecting on the Reading (page 35)

If students have done the activity outlined above, question 1 is a good follow-up activity and a lead-in to class discussion.

Question 4 can be developed into a writing assignment to be done either in class or at home.

Reading 4 (page 36)

To Be Alive Again *Jian Feng (Jimmy) Ye*

In addition to the prereading question on page 36, the teacher can write the title of the essay on the board and then have the students guess what the essay will be about. Responses to the guesses can be recorded on the board as well. After students have read the essay, the teacher can return to these responses to see how closely they correspond to the ideas in the actual essay.

Reflecting on the Reading   (page 37)

Question 3 asks about the word *cherish*, and the activity lends itself to reflection and discussion of the meaning of this word in relation to one's own life. This question can also lead into a discussion of the value of writing a conclusion at the end of an essay. In this case, the author, rather than simply ending the narrative, comments on the fact that he came to realize that his life was irreplaceable, unlike a wristwatch or other material thing. Remind students when writing experiential essays of this kind to be sure to include a conclusion of at least two sentences to provide closure to the essay. Students can conclude by telling the reader what they have learned from an experience or what they hope the reader might learn.

Reading 5   (page 38)

Exodus   *Xiao Mei Sun*

Before reading the essay, students might do some preliminary research either in the library or online about the Cultural Revolution in China in order to provide some historical context. This can be done most easily by entering the keywords *China Cultural Revolution* in any popular search engine. (Note that researching *China Cultural Revolution* online is also an option in the *Internet Search* activity for this chapter on page 49.) Alternatively, the teacher can bring in a brief article about this period either as a pre- or postreading supplement.

Reflecting on the Reading   (page 41)

In question 1, students are asked to examine a list and then choose which items they think the rain symbolizes in the essay. Perhaps due to the experience of taking multiple-choice tests, students have a tendency to think that there can be only one correct answer. However, in this case, any or all of the answers could be correct, provided that the students can find evidence in the text to support their interpretations. A variety of answers can lead to interesting class discussions as well.

Reading 6   (page 41)

The Photograph   *Sha Sha Chen*

Ask students to freewrite briefly about the prereading question. Be sure they save this writing in their notebooks because they may find they can use it as the basis for the *Essay Assignment* in this chapter on page 50.

When asked to interpret a piece of writing, students often feel that their own ideas are not authoritative unless they agree with the teacher's interpretation. However, in this essay, there really is no right or wrong interpretation as even the author herself was not sure as to some of the details of the story. It is therefore important, especially in answering questions 1 and 2, that students be given free rein to explore different interpretations of the text. The goal is not to find the "right" interpretation but to find details in the text to support a point of view.

TECHNIQUES WRITERS USE (pages 44–48)

This section of each chapter provides activities that serve as prewriting exercises for the chapter's *Essay Assignment*.

Memory Chain (page 44)

This technique can be used effectively to stimulate memories that can then be developed into writing topics. Although some narratives center around life-or-death crises, it is important for students to realize that even the simple experiences of daily life can become interesting writing topics.

Task 2.1 *Analyze* (page 44)

Answers may vary. The purpose of this task is to demonstrate the value of a memory chain in helping to recall, organize, and develop ideas from memory.

Task 2.2 *Practice* (page 45)

For this task, as with most tasks in the book, modeling the task for the students is recommended. If possible, prepare a memory chain in advance based on personal experience and then develop the memory chain into a narrative essay. In the classroom, write the original memory chain on the board and then explain to the students the associations that led to the finished essay, which can be shared with the class. An alternative is to have students complete the steps of the task and choose a good example of a student's memory chain. Discuss this with the class before sharing the student's essay based on this chain.

Time Chunks (page 46)

This technique offers another way to generate and organize a narrative following a chronological outline.

Task 2.3 *Analyze* (page 46)

The purpose of this task is to make students aware of the structure of a chronological essay and also to see how the chunking outline helped the writer organize the essay.

Practice (page 48)

Modeling this task before assigning it is recommended. Develop a finished narrative, and then share the writing process with the class.

INTERNET SEARCH (pages 49–50)

This section in Part II (Chapters 2–4) provides activities related to the readings that help students develop their Internet research skills. In Part III (Chapters 5–7), the *Internet Search* is directly related to the chapter's *Essay Assignment*.

Teachers may want to look at A *Word of Caution About the Internet* on page 28 of this manual before introducing students to the *Internet Search*. We suggest waiting to discuss this cautionary advice with students until Chapter 4 – the first time students are asked to do some writing directly related to their Internet research – but some teachers may want to make their students aware of the issues now.

Task 2.5 *Practice* (page 49)

In situations where computer images are able to be projected onto a screen, it may be useful to model one or two sample searches and then discuss with students which of the search results is most relevant to the essays they are reading. In situations in which students do not have ready access to the Internet, do some sample searches in advance and bring in printouts for the class to discuss in groups as they would in questions 3, 4, and 5 on page 50.

ESSAY ASSIGNMENT (pages 50–51)

If students have already completed the *Memory Chain* or *Time Chunks* activities or any of the *Reflecting on the Reading* activities in this chapter, they may use these as the basis for this writing assignment. If not, it might be useful to have students try one of these techniques prior to starting this assignment. You might also model this assignment by bringing in some samples of other successful student narratives, some samples of published writing, or your own narrative writing. A discussion of what makes these samples successful will help students understand what qualities you expect to see in their writing.

Writing Tips (page 50)

Consider asking the students to read these tips silently and then discuss with a partner or a group which ones they think are most important and why.

Writing Your First Draft (page 51)

Not all students will be familiar with the word *draft*. Many students are used to writing only a single draft and may not be experienced in revising their work. It may be useful at this point to explain what a draft is and how, in order to produce good writing, skillful writers generally produce more than one draft. This technique is necessary not only to correct errors but also to develop ideas, to improve organization, and to clarify ideas. The following overview can help illustrate this process.

An Overview of the Writing Process

* *Prewriting*
  During this phase students choose or clarify topics and formulate ideas by brainstorming, reading, doing research, discussing, making notes, creating outlines, freewriting, or making diagrams. (Part I: Starting Out contains several techniques and activities for prewriting.)

* *Drafting*
  Students begin to put down on paper the ideas developed during the prewriting phase. The main emphasis at this stage is to capture ideas quickly without undue attention to organization and accuracy of grammar, spelling, and punctuation. Although these aspects of writing are important, they will be taken up during the editing stage, after the ideas are more fully developed.

* *Revising*
  After sharing their first drafts with the teacher, a peer, or a tutor, students are encouraged to focus on such issues as clarity; organization of ideas; development of a thesis; the inclusion of illustrations and examples; the use of an introduction, body, and conclusion; and, in some cases, the need to do more research. A draft may go through several revisions before it reaches the editing stage. (The peer response activities in Chapters 2 through 7 facilitate revising.)

* *Editing*
  After one or more rounds of revising, students can begin to focus intensively on accuracy of grammar, spelling, punctuation, and mechanics. Students should think of this phase of the process as "washing the window." That is, no matter how beautiful the view is outside your window, if the glass is streaked or dirty, people tend to notice the dirt rather than the view. If the essay has a lot of grammatical and mechanical errors, the reader will focus on the errors as opposed to the ideas. (Chapters 2 through 7 conclude with sections on *Editing Your Essay* that provide an *Editing Checklist*, which students can use independently or with a teacher, peer, or tutor.)

* *Publishing*
  There are many ways of publishing student writing. These include photocopying an essay for the class, projecting an essay using an overhead or computer projector, creating a student magazine, or creating online journals. Publishing can be a great motivator as it encourages students to write for an audience. The process of preparing work for publication creates a natural desire to make it as good as possible.

REVISING YOUR ESSAY (pages 51–54)

In addition to reviewing the questions on page 51, consider showing a few samples of student essays before and after revising. We recommend that before sharing these samples, the teacher corrects all the grammatical errors in both drafts so that students can focus on how the ideas and details of the essay have changed from draft to draft. It is important to emphasize here that while grammar, spelling, and punctuation are important, they are only important so as not to interfere with the understanding and presentation of the content of the essay. A boring and undeveloped essay will still be a poor piece of writing, even if it is grammatically perfect.

Peer Response (page 52)

Some students will already be used to peer response activities; however, others may not have done them before. It is important to structure these response activities very carefully and, whenever possible, to model the types of peer interaction expected. Explain the value and importance of getting feedback from more than one person before beginning a peer response activity. The *Ground Rules for Peer Response* on page 53 are also important in helping students know what is expected of them.

Oral Peer Response (page 53)

In this chapter, students are introduced to the peer response process through oral peer response. In Chapter 3, students will begin to practice written peer response.

Writing Your Second Draft (page 54)

Impress on students that although they should seriously consider the feedback they have received from their peers, they must decide for themselves which peer comments are valuable and which are not.

EDITING YOUR ESSAY (pages 54–58)

It is important for students to understand that grammatical correctness is only one component of good writing and that revision of ideas, organization, and clarity usually come first. However, the editing stage is the time to focus on grammatical correctness.

Begin this section by reading through *What Is Editing?* and *What Is Proofreading?* with the students and answering any questions they may have. You will probably want to review *What Is Proofreading?* with them before they use the *Editing Checklist* on page 58.

Grammar in Context: Using Verb Tenses Correctly (page 56)

The *Grammar in Context* sections of *In Your Own Words* provide a brief review of issues in grammar that are typically problematic for students. For a more detailed analysis of usage, refer students to a grammar reference book or an online resource.

The activities in this section are designed to heighten awareness of verb tenses as used in personal narratives. The simple present tense is often used for making generalizations or descriptions in introductions of current conditions. For example, "Overpopulation is a serious problem in many parts of the world." It is also used in conclusions such as "In order to solve the problem of overpopulation, people need to be educated about family planning." The simple past tense is most often used for personal narratives and specific examples, especially those drawn from personal experience. For example, in an essay about overpopulation, the writer may shift to past tense to relate the following example, "When I was visiting the city of Shanghai, I was amazed to see how crowded the buses were. People were literally pressed together so tightly it was difficult to breathe." The important thing to remember is that verb tenses should generally be consistent, and if one does shift tenses, it should be for a reason.

Task 2.6 *Analyze* (page 56)

In response to the second part of question 1, most of the verbs are in the past tense. The author chose this tense to give the sense of an experience from another place and time.

For question 2, the author switches back and forth between past and present tenses. She uses present tense to convey a sense of action taking place to put the reader into the scene. She uses past tense to step back from the action and describe from a distance what happened.

Segment	When Events Occurred (past or present)	Basic Verb Tense
Paragraphs 1–6	*past*	*present*
Paragraphs 7–27	*present*	*present*
Paragraphs 25–36	*past*	*past*

For question 3, the writer switches back to the present tense to describe the way things stand today with her father.

After discussing question 4, students might try rewriting sections of the essay using different verb tenses to see what the effects are.

Task 2.7 *Practice* (page 57)

See the *Answer Key* on page 257 of the Student's Book.

Editing Checklist (page 58)

You will probably want to review *What Is Proofreading?* on page 55 with students before they complete the checklist. Stress the value of proofreading three separate times, each time with a different objective.

Chapter 3 People

READINGS (pages 60–72)

The six student essays in this chapter include reminiscences, character sketches, and personal memoirs about people. These readings are presented to show students various ways of writing about people who have influenced the writers deeply.

Reading 1 (page 60)

My Grandmother *Hikaru Takahashi*

As an alternative to the prereading exercise, students might be asked to write down and discuss some conflicts that occur between parents and their adult children. The following categories may help elicit student ideas: love, money, career, and education. The list of conflicts can then be summarized on the board. After students have read the essay, return to the list of conflicts and see which occurred in the essay.

An additional option is to have the students examine the photograph of the kabuki actor on page 59. On the blackboard, make a list of four or five descriptive headings such as physical description, time and place, association, and mood. Then ask the students to write corresponding responses to these questions: *What do you see in the picture? In which country do you think this picture was taken, and when was it taken? What does the picture remind you of? How does the picture make you feel?* After reading each question, pause for a minute or two while the students write their responses. When most of the students seem to be finished, go on to the next question. Write or have a designated student write brief summaries of student responses under the headings on the board. These can be revisited after the reading to examine any connections to the text.

Reflecting on the Reading (page 61)

In response to question 1, most students choose b.

For question 2, the grandmother's decision to disobey her parents, leave home, and become an actress are all examples of independence. The decision to accept an arranged marriage, leave the theater, and move to the countryside are examples of the grandmother giving up her independence.

For question 3, there are direct quotations in paragraphs 5, 6, and 8 that reveal the grandmother's talent, success, independence, and dignity.

Question 4 lends itself to the development of a biographical essay.

Reading 2 (page 62)

My Mother *Eileen Peng*

For the prereading activity, read the first four paragraphs aloud to ensure that the students do not proceed too far into the essay before making their predictions.

Reflecting on the Reading (page 63)

For question 1, examples of words that describe the mother's character are *capable* and *lively* (Par. 5) and *good housewife* (Par. 6).

Possible answers to the first part of question 2 are that other people comment on the mother's ability to ride a bicycle fast (Par. 3) and on her ability to further the author's education (Par. 11). These details reveal her capability and devotion to her children's education.

Question 3 lends itself to more in-depth discussion. It can also be followed up with a mini-research activity in which students search for information on the traditional roles of men and women either in Chinese society or in their own cultures.

Question 4 lends itself to the development of an essay writing assignment.

Reading 3 (page 64)

Rosita *Gloria Cortes*

When asked to write biographical essays, most students tend to idealize the people they write about. In this essay, the writer has chosen to write about someone for whom she had extremely negative feelings. You could point out that a lot of great writing deals with conflict and unhappy relationships and that students who feel so inclined might choose to write about such a relationship themselves.

Reflecting on the Reading (page 66)

Any of the answers to question 1 could be correct, provided that students are able to provide evidence in the text to support their point of view.

For question 2, there are numerous descriptive details in paragraphs 3, 4, and 5.

In response to question 3, there can be thoughtful disagreements among students as to whether the conclusion is effective.

Question 4 is a follow-up to the prereading question and can also lead toward a writing assignment. Students might think about conflicts they have had with teachers, bosses, school bullies, or ex-friends.

Reading 4 (page 66)

My Father Intissar Haddiya

As an alternative to the prereading activity, rather than asking students to choose only one person who has had an influence on their lives, ask them to list four or five. Then from that list, have them choose the one who was the most influential and explain why.

Reflecting on the Reading (page 67)

Question 3 lends itself to in-depth discussion. As a follow-up, students might be asked to do a mini-research project on attitudes toward psychology within immigrant communities.

Question 4 serves as the follow-up to the prereading question for this essay and could also serve as a prewriting activity for a biographical essay.

Reading 5 (page 68)

My Friend Nafiz Syed R. Saeed

Whenever time permits and at whatever stage of the reading you think appropriate, elicit from students how the photographs in the text relate to the readings. Before beginning this reading, you might ask students what differences they observe between the young men in the photograph on the left and in the photograph on the right. Write the key points from the discussion on the board. Return to them after the students have finished the reading in order to discuss any connections to the text.

As a variation on the prereading question, rather than ask students to list only one person from high school they remember most clearly, ask them to list four or five. Then from that list, have them choose the one who was the most influential and explain why.

Reflecting on the Reading (page 70)

For question 1, the details about Nafiz can be found in paragraph 3.

For question 2, most of the description can be found in paragraph 3. Some possible details might include the way he moved his hands, the absence of a smile, his baggy pants, and his short stature. This question invites students to draw a picture of the character Nafiz from the essay. While some students might welcome this opportunity, others may feel uncomfortable or feel the task is too childish. For this reason, offer students the option of either writing or drawing.

Question 4 could serve as a prewriting activity for a biographical essay.

Reading 6 (page 70)

Teacher, It's Nice to Meet You, Too *Ruby Ibañez*

As an alternative to the prereading exercise, ask students if they know anyone who has been a refugee. If students have not met a refugee, they can instead list some of the challenges faced by immigrants when learning a new language or entering a new culture.

Reflecting on the Reading (page 72)

For questions 1 and 3, as in other multiple-choice questions in this book, any of the answers could be correct as long as students are able to provide evidence in the text to support their points of view.

For question 2, students might actually rewrite a paragraph or two of the essay in third person narrative to illustrate the stylistic differences and effects of first versus third person. First person narrative gives a sense of immediacy to the writing, the feeling that the character is speaking directly to the reader as if in conversation. Third person narrative distances the reader from the action and is better suited for analysis.

Question 4 is a follow-up to the prereading question, but it broadens the question so that students can answer even if they do not know a refugee.

TECHNIQUES WRITERS USE (pages 73–76)

This section presents activities that serve as prewriting tasks for the chapter's *Essay Assignment*.

People Watching (page 73)

This task helps students learn to observe details that can be used in the development of a memorable portrait. Encourage students to use these details to paint a word picture of the person they are describing.

Task 3.1 *Analyze* (page 73)

Examples of details students might underline are: "His white beard had darkened with the grime. . . . His dark, dirty face – unwashed maybe for weeks . . ."

Task 3.2 *Practice* (page 74)

Although this task was designed to be done individually, it can also be done with partners. In this case each pair of students observes the same scene; however, each partner will then write up his or her observations independently. When the students discuss their observations in a group (step 4), it will be interesting for the group to compare and contrast the two observations of the same scene.

Making Metaphors (page 75)

This activity is designed to help students gain an appreciation of the use of effective metaphors in the description of people.

Task 3.3 Analyze (page 75)

The purpose of this task is to demonstrate how metaphors can reveal characteristics of an individual or a relationship. There are no single correct answers for question 2. Any interpretation is acceptable provided the students can support it with evidence from the text.

Task 3.4 Practice (page 76)

If some students find this activity difficult, remind them that this is only one of many ways to prepare for writing an essay and that we can only find out what works for each of us by experimentation.

INTERNET SEARCH (page 77)

Although students are not asked to incorporate the results of their Internet research into their writing until Chapter 4, some students may choose to write their essay assignment for this chapter on someone for whom biographical information is available on the Internet. If that is the case, take the opportunity to review with students the issues presented in *A Word of Caution About the Internet* on page 28 of this manual.

Task 3.5 Practice (page 77)

This activity can be done in a computer lab if the class has access to one or as an out-of-class assignment. Ideally, each student will become an expert about his or her biographical subject and then teach others in the class what he or she has learned. An equally important goal is for students to expand their Internet skills and share their knowledge with their classmates.

In situations where computer images can be projected onto a screen, it may be useful to model one or two sample searches and then discuss with students which of the search results is most relevant to the essays they are reading. Alternatively, the teacher can do some sample searches in advance and bring in printouts for the class to discuss in groups or as a class. The students will then be able to complete steps 4 and 5 using the printouts.

ESSAY ASSIGNMENT (pages 77–79)

After the students have read the assignment, be sure that they review the writing they have already done for this chapter to see if it gives them ideas or could serve as the basis for the *Essay Assignment*.

Writing Tips (page 78)

Detailed tips for writing about people are presented to help students prepare for this assignment.

Writing Your First Draft (page 79)

If necessary, review with students the information in *Writing Your First Draft* on page 14 of this manual.

REVISING YOUR ESSAY (pages 79–82)

Review what is meant by *revising* with the students. For a more detailed explanation, see *An Overview of the Writing Process* on page 15 of this manual.

Written Peer Response (page 79)

In Chapter 2, students responded orally to their peers. In this chapter, they practice giving written feedback on each other's work. To help in modeling the written peer response process, before and after drafts of a student essay are provided on pages 79–81. Requiring students to analyze these drafts critically and to use the *Practice Peer Response Form* on pages 88 and 89 will be extremely useful as a model for the way in which they will evaluate their own drafts in *Responding to Your Peers*, the next activity.

EDITING YOUR ESSAY (pages 82–87)

It is important for students to understand that grammatical correctness is only one component of good writing and that revision of ideas, organization, and clarity usually come first. However, the editing stage is the time to focus on grammatical correctness.

Grammar in Context: Understanding Sentence Boundaries (page 82)

This section contains activities to help students become aware of sentence boundaries as well as the correct use of independent and dependent clauses and associated punctuation.

Task 3.6 *Analyze* (page 85)

See the *Answer Key* on page 258 of the Student's Book.

Task 3.7 *Practice* (page 85)

See the Answer Key on page 258 of the Student's Book.

Editing Checklist (page 87)

If necessary, review *What Is Proofreading?* on page 55 of the Student's Book with students before they complete the checklist. Stress the value of proofreading three separate times, each time with a different objective.

Chapter 4 — Places

READINGS (pages 94–107)

This chapter's readings make use of physical setting as the starting point for narrative writing. The six student essays explore settings of home, village, or native country as vehicles for developing ideas about the relationship between a physical place and the emotions, culture, and lessons that emanate from it.

Reading 1 (page 94)

The Tree of My Secrets *Amalfi Richard*

As a variation on the prereading question on page 94, ask students to think of a place from their childhood and do a free association activity by writing down any thoughts about the place in answer to the following questions: *Where was it? Who was usually there? What did the place look like? What often happened there? How did you feel about the place?* Read the questions aloud, pausing between each one to give students time to write their associations.

Reflecting on the Reading (page 95)

Questions 2 and 3 deal with personification and similes. As a follow-up activity, students might be asked to create similes and metaphors that they could use in describing their own special places.

Reading 2 (page 96)

The Home of My Childhood *Volkan Cinozgumus*

For an alternative to the prereading exercise, ask students to think of a place from their childhoods and then record answers to the following questions:

What did the place look like? What did it smell like? What did people eat and drink there? What was the weather like there? What sounds were there? Read the questions aloud, pausing between each one to give students time to write their associations.

Reflecting on the Reading (page 97)

If students have done the activity outlined above and answered question 1, they can compare their own sensory details to the ones in the essay.

As a variation on question 2, students can rewrite a paragraph or two of the essay, changing the narrative from second person to third person, before they discuss the different effect this would produce.

Question 4 may be used as a prewriting activity for the *Essay Assignment* on page 111.

Reading 3 (page 98)

The Coldest Winter of Beijing *Jian Wei*

Prior to reading this essay, students are asked to think about a political leader who has been influential in their lives. Write the names of such leaders on the board and ask the students to discuss why they were influential.

Reflecting on the Reading (page 100)

There is no one correct answer for question 1. Any answer can be correct, provided that students are able to support it with evidence from the text.

For question 2, there are many details related to the senses in paragraphs 2 and 11.

As a follow-up to question 4, students can be asked to do either online or library research on a political figure from their own country.

Reading 4 (page 100)

Community Culture *Tatyana Sokolovskaya*

Before the reading, students are asked to think about a place they visit when they want to reconnect with their past. If students are not able to think of such a place, they might be asked to think of the neighborhood they like best. If students choose this option, they can begin their freewriting for question 4 of *Reflecting on the Reading* by completing the following sentence: "I like this neighborhood because . . ."

Reflecting on the Reading (page 102)

There is no one right answer for question 1. Any answer can be correct, provided that students are able to support it with evidence from the text.

A Village from the Past *Zhanna Kayumova*

For the prereading exercise, if students are not able to think of a place that was new or strange to them, they might be asked to think about any place they have visited for the first time and to think about what they remember most about it. They might also think about the house of an older relative.

Reflecting on the Reading   (page 104)

Question 2 asks students to bring in a photograph connected with their family's past. As an alternative, students might bring in a special object, book, or other item that connects to their family history.

For Question 3, students are asked to identify details of the story that are seen from the child's perspective as opposed to the details seen from an adult perspective. For example, "In the dark, everything looked different to me, especially the trees" (Par. 3) is an example of the child's point of view. The sentence "Now I feel like I missed something" (Par. 7) is an example of an adult's point of view. A variation on this question might be to have students actually rewrite a paragraph or two from a child's point of view before they discuss the different effect this would produce. Consider modeling this for the students first.

New Horizon of Beauty *Sumiko Masaki*

For the prereading exercise, if students are not able to think of a place that changed their lives, they might be asked to look at the photograph depicting Matisse's Chapel of the Rosary on page 105 and think about these questions: *What do you see in the picture? What feeling or mood do you get from the picture? Do you think you would like to be inside this chapel? Why or why not?*

Reflecting on the Reading   (page 107)

For question 1, some examples of visual imagery are: ". . . the sensitive change of the color of the sky . . ." (Par 1); "Sunshine through the stained glass dyed the white floor yellow, green, and blue" (Par. 7); and "The sea was like a piece of golden cloth" (Par. 9).

For question 4, if students are not able to think of a specific place that changed their lives, they might be asked to write about a famous place they have visited, a building either in their hometown or neighborhood, or the home of a close friend or relative.

TECHNIQUES WRITERS USE (pages 107–110)

This section presents activities that serve as prewriting tasks for the chapter's *Essay Assignment*.

Appealing to All the Senses (page 107)

Task 4.1 *Analyze* (page 107)

For question 1, sensory details include ads (sight), perfume (smell), fresh-printed newspapers (smell), wet coats (smell), and the sound of the train (hearing).

In response to question 3, students should note that when the writer closed his eyes, he became more aware of the smells and sounds that surrounded him.

Task 4.2 *Practice* (page 108)

As a variation, students can be assigned to do this activity in pairs. Each partner can write up his or her observation individually. When the students return to class, the two observations can be compared to see how they were similar or different.

Using Memories from the Past (page 108)

Task 4.3 *Analyze* (page 108)

In response to question 3, there is no correct answer. However, students should be able to back up their opinions with examples from the text.

Task 4.4 *Practice* (page 109)

This task encourages students to practice using sensory details to *show* rather than *tell* their story.

INTERNET SEARCH (pages 110–111)

In this activity, students are asked to research their hometowns or cities. In some cases there may not be much information available about a specific town, especially if it is a very small town. In such cases, direct students to search for information on the nearest city to their town or on the state or province in which their town is located.

Task 4.5 *Practice* (page 110)

Since this is the first task in which students are asked to do some writing using the information they retrieved in their Internet searches, it may be a good time to discuss with them some or all of the issues below.

A Word of Caution About the Internet

- *Plagiarism*
  Due to the ready availability of online sources, including downloadable prepackaged research papers, teachers need to be aware that some students may be tempted to plagiarize. For this reason, teachers must make it very clear to their students that cutting and pasting material from the Internet or copying material from any sources without proper citation is unacceptable in any academic setting. If a teacher suspects that a student has copied material from the Internet, one way of tracing the material to its source is simply to copy an exact sentence, preferably a sentence containing unusual or sophisticated syntax or vocabulary, into the search box of any major search engine. If the passage was copied from any online source, the search engine should be able to identify the source very quickly. The teacher can then notify the student of the plagiarism and take appropriate action. In addition, even if students successfully paraphrase source material, they should be made aware that any information, data, or opinions need to be cited properly.

- *Evaluating Web Sites*
  Besides the obvious problem of plagiarism, there is also a tendency for students to accept uncritically the accuracy and legitimacy of any Web sites they happen to come across. It is important for teachers to help students distinguish between reliable, objective sources of information and those that are less professional or whose information is biased according to a political agenda or motivated by a commercial objective. There are numerous rubrics available to evaluate the reliability of Web sites on the Internet. These can be found by entering the keywords *Web site assessment* in any major search engine. If time permits, invite a librarian to share Internet searching skills with the class.

- *Avoiding Offensive Material*
  Teachers should be aware that students may encounter highly offensive or pornographic material while performing a legitimate academic search. If at all possible, the teacher should model some sample searches with the students, preferably by using a computer projector that can show the actual results of a search inquiry. The teacher can then help students to see which sites might best be avoided.

ESSAY ASSIGNMENT (pages 111–112)

After the students have read the assignment, be sure that they review the writing they have already done for this chapter to see if it gives them ideas or could serve as the basis for the *Essay Assignment*.

Writing Tips (page 111)

Detailed tips for writing about places are presented to help students prepare for this assignment.

Writing Your First Draft (page 112)

If necessary, review with students the information in *Writing Your First Draft* on page 14 of this manual.

REVISING YOUR ESSAY (pages 112–115)

Review what is meant by *revising* with the students. For a more detailed explanation, see *An Overview of the Writing Process* on page 15 of this manual.

In *Giving More Helpful Peer Response*, students should be guided toward understanding that the more useful written response is by Student B.

Writing Your Second Draft (page 115)

Impress on students that although they should seriously consider the feedback they have received from their peers, they must decide for themselves which peer comments are valuable and which are not.

EDITING YOUR ESSAY (pages 115–118)

It is important for students to understand that grammatical correctness is only one component of good writing and that revision of ideas, organization, and clarity usually come first. However, once students arrive at the editing stage, they must focus on grammatical correctness.

Grammar in Context: Using the Plural Form of Nouns (page 115)

There are several possible causes of errors related to the plural endings of nouns. In some languages, such as Chinese, nouns are not usually marked with plural endings if it is clear from the context that more than one object is being discussed. For example, a literal translation of Chinese would be *ige bi* – one pen, *liange bi* – two pen. However, this does not explain errors made by speakers of languages that do mark the plural endings of nouns, such as Spanish. These errors may be caused because in spoken English nonnative speakers do not always hear the -s ending clearly. For example, a student might write, "He own three house." Some students may actually drop -s and -ed endings off words in their speech, and this pattern is then replicated in their writing. The problem is further complicated by the irregular plural forms, such as *woman–women*. It is difficult for students to hear the difference. While this type of singular/plural error may go unnoticed in informal speech situations, students need to become aware that missing or incorrect noun forms stand out in formal writing and distract from the ideas in an essay. This is why proofreading and editing for these types of errors is important.

Task 4.6 *Analyze* (page 116)

See the *Answer Key* on page 259 of the Student's Book.

Task 4.7 *Practice* (page 117)

See the *Answer Key* on page 259 of the Student's Book.

Editing Checklist (page 118)

If necessary, review *What Is Proofreading?* on page 55 of the Student's Book with students before they complete the checklist. Stress the value of proofreading three separate times, each time with a different objective.

A NOTE BEFORE YOU CONTINUE (page 119)

At this point, students should complete *Assessing Your Progress: A Midterm Survey* on page 122. It is important for students to measure their own progress and also to identify areas that still need work while there is time remaining in the term to address these issues. We recommend that teachers go over these surveys with their students – ideally, in a student-teacher conference – to discuss progress in the course and to identify areas that need improvement. The teacher can also get valuable feedback regarding how students are responding to the course activities.

PART III
MORE FORMAL WRITING

In Part III, students practice more formal writing as they begin to analyze their own experiences and attitudes in the light of larger societal forces.

Chapter 5 serves as a transitional chapter in which students use interviews they have conducted as the base for their analytic essays. They may choose between interviewing someone and writing about a theme in that person's life, or interviewing one or more individuals for information on a topic of interest that will be the focus of their essay. In this chapter, students are introduced to the traditional academic practice of formulating a thesis statement.

In Chapter 6, students write traditional reading-based essays using one or more print sources from the chapter. The topic is one familiar to every college student: how families are changing in the modern world. Not only do students comment on their print sources, they must also summarize and paraphrase ideas from these sources.

In Chapter 7, students write a brief research paper that includes identification of their sources according to APA or MLA style. As in the previous chapters, the topics are of high interest: (1) the influence of such factors as race, ethnicity, and immigration status on the formation of personal identity, and (2) an assessment of the possible advantages and disadvantages of interracial marriage. Students are required to use at least three research sources, one of which must be a reading in the chapter, another from the Internet, and a third that includes statistical information. They are encouraged to consider articles, books, and journals for their sources as well as personally conducted interviews.

Oral History
Writing Based on Interviews

Chapter
5

The readings and activities in this chapter are based on interviews, or oral histories. The techniques used are derived from ethnographic research – a form of qualitative research widely used in the social sciences as a way of interpreting the culture of a society by observing and interviewing individual members of that society.

READINGS (pages 128–145)

This chapter contains five oral histories by student writers in the form of interviews for life history projects. These student writers interviewed older relatives and friends, obtaining fascinating stories about the interrelationship between family history and the social, political, and cultural movements of world history. The last reading in the chapter is an oral history of a young immigrant from India who describes his narrow escape from the collapse of the World Trade Center in New York on September 11, 2001.

Reading 1 (page 128)

A Reward from Buddha *Zhong Chen*

As a variation on the prereading question, students might be asked to make a list of four or five older people they would like to interview. They can be older relatives, family friends, or even former teachers. Students can then pick from the list one person they think would be most interesting.

Reflecting on the Reading (page 130)

For question 1, there is no right answer. Any interpretation should be acceptable, provided students are able to support it in the text.

In question 3, fourteen of the twenty-five paragraphs have direct quotations, ten of which are from Chen's great-uncle. There are various ways to mix direct and indirect quotations in essays, but what students should notice is that usually a mixture of the two types of quotations helps to make the essay interesting. Students should also notice that the interviewer, Chen, speaks considerably less than the interviewee, his great-uncle. As a follow-up activity, students might be asked to rewrite a brief section of the essay, changing all the direct quotations to indirect quotations or vice versa.

Reading 2 (page 131)

Unfinished Interview *Tatyana Dyachenko*

As preparation to or as follow-up for this reading, students might be asked to think about the kinds of problems or dangers civilians might face during wartime. Students can then see how many of these problems appear in the reading.

Reflecting on the Reading (page 133)

A possible answer to question 1 would be: This is an essay about a woman's tremendous strength that enabled her to survive against all odds.

The references to food mentioned in question 2 relate to the experience of starvation during the war in which many thousands of people died. People who have lived through a period of starvation often become obsessed with food.

Question 3 addresses two kinds of direct quotations, those the mother said during the interview and quotes that are recalled by the author. For example, the mother says, "Have you already had your breakfast?" in paragraph 2. This is an example of the first type of quotation. In paragraph 7, the question "Have you already eaten something today?" is an example of a quotation that did not come from the interview but was recalled by the author.

Reading 3 (page 134)

My First Interview Larisa Zubataya

As preparation for this reading, students might be asked to discuss the meaning of the word *prejudice*. The definition can be written on the board. After the reading, students can return to the definition and look for examples of prejudice in the text.

Reflecting on the Reading (page 136)

Question 2 lends itself to a discussion of the nature of prejudice and whether it is learned behavior or perhaps in some ways a part of nature.

For question 3, it is recommended that students write down a few possible topics, and then choose one that they would like to investigate more thoroughly. The teacher can model this process. For example, to investigate the topic "The Causes of Poverty," the researcher might ask the following questions: *What is the definition of poverty? Is poverty a natural or man-made condition? Why are some parts of the world so much poorer than others? Why are some people so much poorer than others? Is education the best cure for poverty?*

As a follow-up to question 4, ask students to do a mini-research project on the history of any of the groups they identified as being scapegoats.

Reading 4 (page 137)

Interview with Andrei Young Ja Lee

As a prereading activity, ask students to make a list of some of the difficulties immigrants might face when coming to a new country for the first time. Write these on the board. After the reading, return to this list and have the class determine which of these challenges Andrei faced.

Reflecting on the Reading (page 138)

As a follow-up to question 1, ask students to rewrite a paragraph or two of the interview, converting direct quotations to indirect ones or vice versa.

Examples of possible answers to question 2 are: "He replied quickly with a slight tinge of impatience . . ." (Par. 7) and "His voice became sharp" (Par. 9).

(page 139)

One of Us Ahmet Erdogan

For the prereading activity, write the title "One of Us" on the board and then tell the class they are going to read an interview with a homeless person. Ask the students to predict what the title might mean. Then record the predictions on the board and return to them after the students have read the essay to see how accurate they were.

Reflecting on the Reading   (page 142)

In answer to question 1, the author uses the first two paragraphs to point out the prejudice that exists toward homeless people in society.

For question 2, students may observe that the author's attitude changes from one of disgust to one of sympathy.

Reading 6 (page 142)

An Immigrant's First Day on the Job

Saravanan Rangaswamy, as told to Dean E. Murphy

The prereading activity assumes that most students using the book will have a clear memory of what took place on September 11, 2001. However, as time passes, it may be necessary to review the facts of what happened that day.

Reflecting on the Reading   (page 145)

For question 2, students are asked to note the details related to the passage of time. This is important because these details help to create a historical record of what happened. For example, we can match the time sequence described in the oral history with other officially recorded events, such as the exact moment the planes struck the towers or the moment each tower began to collapse.

As a follow-up to question 2, students can do some research on the details provided during the interviews. For example, many of the Web sites devoted to 9/11 offer very detailed time lines that students can compare to the sequence of events Rangaswamy describes.

For question 3, all the descriptors – terror, courage, gratitude, and determination – may accurately describe the narrator's feelings at various points in his narration. For example, he experienced terror when he heard the explosion but later felt gratitude toward the people who helped him survive.

TECHNIQUES WRITERS USE (pages 146–151)

This section presents activities that serve as prewriting tasks for the chapter's *Essay Assignment*.

Interviewing (page 146)

A list of specific guidelines is provided to help students get started on an interviewing assignment. Go over these techniques with the class before they begin the tasks.

Task 5.1 *Analyze* (page 146)

For question 2, students identify short-answer and open-ended questions. For example, "Can you describe your childhood in the village?" is an open-ended question because it encourages the interviewee to speak freely and at length. On the other hand, "How many children did you have?" is a closed question as it calls for a specific, brief answer.

Question 3 is designed to illustrate the importance of direct quotations in revealing the personality of the interviewee.

In question 4, students might point out the importance of open-ended and closed questions to elicit a broad overview as well as specific detail. They might also discuss the use of direct and indirect quotation to capture the voice of the subject.

Task 5.2 *Practice* (page 148)

In this task, students conduct practice interviews with partners as preparation for interviews to be conducted outside the classroom.

Formulating a Thesis Statement (page 148)

It is a good idea to take plenty of time to discuss thesis statements because formulating them will be required of students in many academic writing situations.

Task 5.3 *Analyze* (page 149)

In question 1, c and d meet the criteria for a thesis statement because both express an opinion that is arguable and supportable. For example, in statement c the writer can support the idea that American culture is youth oriented by citing data such as statistics on consumer spending by young people or on the typical age range of television viewers. To support the opinion that older people are not respected, the writer can find research that gives examples of neglect of the elderly by some families or in some nursing homes. Regarding statement d, the writer can use statistics to support the opinion that a larger portion of the population is becoming elderly. The second part of d – whether or not old people will gain more respect – is not easily supported by statistics, but it might be supported by examples and is certainly arguable. Statements a and b simply state facts but do not indicate a hypothesis that can be supported by data.

Task 5.4 Practice (page 150)

To determine if the criteria for a thesis statement have been met, students should ask themselves: *Does the statement express my opinion on the topic? Is my statement arguable? That is, is it possible for someone to disagree with my statement? Can I provide evidence such as statistics, examples, or reasoning to back up my ideas?*

Clustering (page 150)

Explain that the purpose of *clustering* (sometimes called *mapping*) is to help generate and organize ideas for an essay assignment. It is especially helpful for visual learners.

Task 5.5 Analyze (page 151)

The topic of this cluster diagram is "my grandmother's life." The subtopics are "Character," "Lifestyle," "Family," and "Education." The remaining circles provide details of the subtopics.

Task 5.6 Practice (page 151)

Students create their own clustering diagrams using the sample topics in Task 5.4 on page 150. A variation on this task would be to have students generate their own topics.

INTERNET SEARCH (pages 151–153)

The Internet searches students do in Chapters 5, 6, and 7 are directly linked to the *Essay Assignments* for the chapters. (See A *Word of Caution About the Internet* on page 28 of this manual.)

ESSAY ASSIGNMENT (pages 153–157)

In this section of Chapters 5, 6, and 7, guidelines for *Generating Ideas*, *Organizing Ideas*, and *Working Toward a Thesis Statement* are provided for each of the two essay options.

Writing Tips (page 156)

These tips are specifically designed for essays based on interviews. Once the students have completed a first draft of their essays, they might revisit these tips by turning them into questions. For example: *Have I included specific details that reveal my interviewee's character and opinions? Have I varied my use of direct and indirect quotations? Have I introduced quotations with my own words?*

Writing Your First Draft (page 157)

If necessary, review with students the information in *Writing Your First Draft* on page 14 of this manual.

REVISING YOUR ESSAY (pages 157–158)

Review what is meant by *revising* with the students. For a more detailed explanation, see *An Overview of the Writing Process* on page 15 of this manual.

Be sure to review the information in *Making a Plan for Revising* on page 157 with students. In previous chapters, we have advised teachers to remind students that each of them is ultimately responsible for his or her own work, although feedback from peers – and possibly from teachers – is important and helpful. In this chapter, *Writer's Plan for Revising*, a form to help students' plan how to revise their essays is introduced.

Writing Your Second Draft (page 158)

Make sure that students fill out the *Writer's Plan for Revising* form on page 165 before beginning their second draft. Remind them that although they should seriously consider the feedback they have received from their peers, they must decide for themselves which peer comments are useful and which are not.

EDITING YOUR ESSAY (pages 158–161)

It is important for students to understand that grammatical correctness is only one component of good writing and that revision of ideas, organization, and clarity usually come first. However, the editing stage is the time to focus on grammatical correctness.

Grammar in Context: Using Direct and Indirect Quotations (page 158)

Students have a tendency to omit quotation marks in direct quotes or to use the present tense in indirect quotes. They need to be exposed to a variety of correct uses and practice each kind of quotation extensively in their own writing before they will be able to master the forms.

Task 5.7 *Analyze* (page 159)

See the *Answer Key* on page 260 of the Student's Book.

Task 5.8 *Practice* (page 160)

This task provides an enjoyable way for students to practice writing both direct and indirect quotations.

Editing Checklist (page 161)

If necessary, review *What Is Proofreading?* on page 55 of the Student's Book with students before they complete the checklist. Stress the value of proofreading three separate times, each time with a different objective.

Families in Transition
Writing Based on Reading

In Chapter 6, students write a traditional reading-based essay using one or more print sources from the chapter. The topic is one familiar to every college student: how families are changing in the modern world. Not only do students comment on their print sources, but they must also summarize and paraphrase ideas from these sources.

READINGS (pages 168–185)

This chapter contains writing by both students and professional writers who offer a variety of cultural, social, and political analyses of changes taking place in family life around the world.

In this chapter, the controversial topic of same-sex parenting is approached by introducing an article by professional journalist Carlyle Murphy along with student reactions, both pro and con. By introducing controversial topics, we hope to engender debate and encourage students to develop their own opinions and express them – and the reasons for them – in writing.

Reading 1 (page 168)

Traditional vs. Modern Family *Wan L. Lam*

Be aware that students who have experienced or know of extended families tend to think of a traditional family as one in which more than two generations live together, often with such relatives as uncles, aunts, or cousins. On the other hand, students who have only experienced nuclear families or who have grown up in single-parent families may think of the traditional family as a household consisting of two parents and their children. It is important to recognize that terms like *traditional* and *modern* are relative and understood differently in different contexts.

Reflecting on the Reading (page 169)

For question 1, some examples of traditional family structure that appear in the essay are the preference of male to female babies (Par. 2), the subservience of women (Par. 4), and the dominance of men (Par. 4). Some examples of modern family structure include the move out of the old building (Par. 6), the sharing of housework (Par. 6), and the ability of the children to make their own decisions (Par. 7).

For question 2, the answers are as follows:

Category	Traditional	Modern
Where family members live	*All together*	*Only parents and children live together*
The role of men	*Dominant, controlling*	*Equal to women*
The role of women	*Passive, subservient*	*Equal to men*
Attitudes toward the elderly	*Obedient*	*Respectful but not controlling*
Relationship between parents and children	*Obedient, strict*	*more democratic*

As a follow-up to question 4, students can go to encyclopedia articles on the family. There is also a wealth of sociological and anthropological material available online by typing the keywords *traditional family* and *modern family* in any major search engine. This information can be used in developing for Option 1 of the essay assignment on page 194.

Reading 2 (page 170)

The Family in Society *Isabella Kong*

This essay was written as a reaction to the essay by Wan Lam, on page 168.

Reflecting on the Reading   (page 171)

In answer to question 1, examples of why the traditional Chinese family was useful are to prevent the splitting up of the land (Par. 2) and to defend the family from outside threats with the strong union of family members (Par. 3). Reasons why the traditional family is no longer useful can include the ideas that disputes and conflicts often occur among family members (Par. 3) and that individualism and equality are the prevailing ideas in modern society (Par. 4).

As a follow-up to question 3, students might be asked to find other definitions of culture in encyclopedias, dictionaries, or online.

Question 4 invites students to relate personal experiences to this topic; however, bear in mind that not all students will be willing to write about discord within their own families.

Reading 3 (page 171)

Traditional Family and Modern Society in Africa

Papa Aly Ndaw

This essay is closely related to the essay by Lam, on page 168, and the one by Kong, on page 170.

Reflecting on the Reading   (page 173)

In answer to question 1, the two major changes are in family size (Par. 4) and in the increasing rights of family members (Par. 5).

In question 2, guessing is emphasized because it encourages students to use the context to get meaning from the text. Vocabulary that is acquired in context is often more readily acquired in long-term memory than vocabulary that is memorized in isolation.

Reading 4 (page 174)

Bean Paste vs. Miniskirts: Generation Gap Grows

Nicholas D. Kristof

Attempt to answer the prereading question before asking students to think about it. This allows you to consider and then model the kinds of categories associated with cultural change. You might compare gender roles, politics, economics, technology, or social mores as they existed 50 years ago compared with those of today. For example, in the United States in the 1950s, very few women were in high-level careers or ran for public office, and the economy was dominated by major manufacturing corporations such as car makers and steel producers.

Reflecting on the Reading   (page 176)

The primary objective of question 1 is to point out the journalistic technique of piquing the reader's interest by introducing a personal detail or story. Some students may want to experiment with this technique in their own essay writing.

Question 2 is designed to point out how the older generation may object to a loss of national identity among the younger generation.

Question 3 draws students' attention to the use of quotations that illustrate a variety of ideas and emotions. After identifying the appropriate quotations, students can be asked to read aloud the quotations that illustrate the actions or emotions expressed.

a Any quotation from paragraph 2

b Any quotation from paragraph 5

c The quotation in paragraph 6

d The quotation in paragraph 10

The letter-writing activity in question 4 can be applied to almost any of the readings in this book, and it is an excellent way of encouraging students to focus on details in the text as they consider a point of view that is not their own.

Reading 5 (page 177)

A Response to "Bean Paste vs. Miniskirts" *Liana Salman*

This essay was written as a reaction to the article by Kristof, on page 174.

Reflecting on the Reading (page 179)

For question 1, there can be more than one interpretation regarding the main topic in each paragraph. Some students may focus on the ideas being expressed by the interviewees. Others may focus on the opinion expressed by the writer. In either case, students should be asked to explain their choices by pointing to specific details in the text.

For question 2, some examples of summary can be found in paragraphs 1 through 5. Examples of the writer's own opinion can be found in paragraphs 6 and 7. As a follow-up to question 2, students might be asked to summarize a brief passage from the reading in their own words.

Before answering question 3, students should review *Formulating a Thesis Statement*, on page 148. The writer expresses her opinion most directly in paragraph 7: "I believe that younger generations have lost and gained something by giving up old values." If students choose a different paragraph or statement, they should be able to explain their choices.

Reading 6 (page 179)

Gay Parents Find More Acceptance *Carlyle Murphy*

As a variation on the prereading activity, students can be asked to brainstorm the arguments for and against same-sex parenting. This can be done by having half the class think of the arguments in favor while the other half considers the arguments against. The teacher can then record these ideas on the board and return to them after the reading to see which were discussed in the text.

Reflecting on the Reading (page 182)

For question 1, if students have done the pro and con brainstorming activity above, they can match the quotations in the article to those opinions.

A follow-up activity to question 2 is to have students do some research either in the library or online to find out what is known about the causes of sexual preference or identity.

Either the interview activity in question 3 or the letter in question 4 can be developed into a more formal essay.

Reading 7 (page 183)

The Problem of Gay Parenting *Pui Man Wong*

This reading is a response to the article by Carlyle Murphy, on page 179.

Reflecting on the Reading (page 183)

Question 1 is designed to point out the rhetorical technique of anticipating an opposing point of view and answering it. An example is in paragraph 2, when the author points out how gay parenting is becoming more acceptable in modern society. Then in paragraphs 3 and 4 she discusses her own opinion, which is opposed to gay parenting. Ask the students to consider the value of including an opposing point of view in their essays. As a follow-up, have students practice this technique of introducing an opinion that is not their own and then responding to it.

Question 3 emphasizes the importance of properly acknowledging and citing sources.

A variation on question 4 would be to have the students write a letter to a same-sex couple considering adoption or to Carlyle Murphy, author of the article "Gay Parents Find More Acceptance," on page 179.

Reading 8 (page 184)

A Positive View of Gay Parenting *Alana Vayntraub*

This reading is a response to the article by Carlyle Murphy, on page 179.

Reflecting on the Reading (page 185)

For question 1, students might underline any of the quotes in paragraph 3 that support the right to same-sex parenting.

For question 3, students may check paragraphs 4, 5, and 6, all of which deal with emotions.

TECHNIQUES WRITERS USE (pages 186–192)

The activities presented in this section are designed to give students practice in summarizing, paraphrasing, and outlining – three skills that will serve them well in all their academic writing.

Summarizing Information from Written Sources (page 186)

Writing good summaries is an important academic skill and takes a lot of practice before it can be mastered. Students often simply copy text rather than summarize it in their own words. They also try to include too much detail instead of emphasizing the main idea of a passage. Criteria for an effective summary are provided on page 186, and a checklist is included in step 5 of Task 6.2, on page 188.

Task 6.1 *Analyze* (page 186)

The purpose of this task is to make students aware of the conventions of summarizing from sources.

Here are the answers for question 2.

a The title of the article is set off by quotation marks.

b The newspaper title is in italics.

c The original paragraph that Salman summarized is paragraph 5 in the Kristof article. She probably chose this article because it provided an overview of the Korean generation gap.

d In paragraphs 2 and 3, Salman quotes statements from the older women quoted in Kristof's article. She probably did this because the statements reflect a conservative attitude that might seem amusing or old-fashioned to a modern reader and therefore highlight the idea of a generation gap.

Task 6.2 *Practice* (page 187)

For this task, step 5 might work better as a partner activity rather than as a small group activity. In addition to the peer exchange, collecting the summaries and offering feedback is also an option.

Paraphrasing Information from Written Sources (page 188)

Although effective paraphrasing is one of the most important skills in academic writing, it is very rarely taught or practiced in writing classes. It is a skill that takes some time to master. It is also important for students to become aware of the difference between paraphrasing and plagiarism. Therefore, try to find ways to make paraphrasing a regular component of the remainder of the course. It is worthwhile to spend some time examining with your students the examples of acceptable and unacceptable paraphrases that are shown on pages 189–190.

Task 6.3 *Analyze* (page 190)

This task points out some common pitfalls of paraphrasing.

See the *Answer Key* on page 260 of the Student's Book.

Task 6.4 *Practice* (Page 191)

Paraphrasing often leads students to plagiarize either intentionally or unintentionally. One of the purposes of this task is to make students aware of what plagiarism is and why they must avoid it. See the warning about plagiarism in *A Word of Caution About the Internet* on page 28 of this manual.

Outlining (page 191)

The format for an outline of a traditional academic essay is provided on page 191. While some teachers require students to create an outline before writing the paper, others prefer to have students create a first draft of the paper and then make an outline of what they have written. In this way, students may see areas where their papers need to be developed or reorganized.

Task 6.5 *Analyze* (page 192)

See the *Answer Key* on page 260 of the Student's Book.

Task 6.6 *Practice* (page 192)

This activity provides the opportunity to practice developing thesis statements and creating an outline. Students should follow the guidelines for thesis statements on page 148 and the outline format on page 191.

INTERNET SEARCH (pages 192–193)

The Internet searches in Option 1 and Option 2 are directly linked to the *Essay Assignments* on pages 194–195. (See *A Word of Caution About the Internet* on page 28 of this manual.)

ESSAY ASSIGNMENT (pages 194–197)

In this section, guidelines for *Generating Ideas, Organizing Ideas*, and *Working Toward a Thesis Statement* are provided for each of the two essay options.

Writing Tips (page 197)

To help students select titles, suggest several titles for an essay and ask students to decide which one is best. Another helpful activity is to have students read an essay without a title, and then have them think of an appropriate one. Similarly, students can be given a sample essay with the conclusion removed and asked to provide their own.

Writing Your First Draft (page 197)

By this stage of the course, all students should be familiar with the process of drafting, revising, and editing. If necessary, review with students the information in *Writing Your First Draft* on page 14 of this manual.

REVISING YOUR ESSAY (pages 198–199)

By this stage of the course, all students should be familiar with the revising process. If necessary, see *An Overview of the Writing Process* on page 15 of this manual.

Benefiting from Teacher Comments (page 198)

Despite the many hours that writing teachers devote to commenting on student papers, not all students actually read these comments. In order to ensure that students are in fact reading the comments, set aside time in class for students to read and respond to teacher comments. This can be done in mini teacher-student conferences or by having students write their responses or questions beneath the teacher's comments on their papers.

Writing Your Second Draft (page 199)

Make sure that students fill out the *Writer's Plan for Revising* form on page 205 before beginning their second draft. Remind them that although they should seriously consider the feedback they have received from their peers, they must decide for themselves which peer comments are useful and which are not.

EDITING YOUR ESSAY (pages 199–201)

By this stage of the course, all students should be familiar with the editing process. If necessary, see *An Overview of the Writing Process* on page 15 of this manual.

Grammar in Context: Using Modal Auxiliaries (page 199)

Modal auxiliaries are used extensively in formal essay writing to express opinions, speculate on possible outcomes, describe imaginary scenarios, and predict the future. Students frequently make errors when using modal phrases, especially when describing hypothetical situations. The activities in this section are designed to help students use modal phrases correctly.

Task 6.7 *Analyze* (page 199)

See the *Answer Key* on page 261 of the Student's Book.

Task 6.8 *Practice* (page 200)

See the *Answer Key* on page 261 of the Student's Book.

Editing Checklist (page 201)

If necessary, review *What Is Proofreading?* on page 55 of the Student's Book with students before they complete the checklist. Stress the value of proofreading three separate times, each time with a different objective.

7

Issues of Identity
Writing Based on Research

In Chapter 7, students write a brief research paper that includes identification of their sources according to APA or MLA style. As in the previous chapters, the topics are of high interest: (1) the influence of such factors as race, ethnicity, and immigration status on the formation of personal identity, and (2) an assessment of the possible advantages and disadvantages of interracial marriage. Students are required to use at least three research sources, one of which must be a reading in the chapter, another from the Internet, and a third that includes statistical information. They are encouraged to consider articles, books, and journals for their sources as well as personally conducted interviews.

READINGS (pages 208–231)

The final chapter includes writing on issues of identity by students and professional writers. The chapter opens with a formal speech to new immigrants presenting the classic American Dream rags-to-riches immigrant story. This is followed by a critique of the speech by a student writer whose experience is quite different from that of the speechwriter. "America 2050: Immigration and the Hourglass," by sociologist Alejandro Portes, points out the obstacles to the American Dream faced by many immigrants.

The second half of the chapter introduces the theme of racial identity with a student essay describing the difficulties faced by a student of mixed race and ethnicity. In her essay "The Color of Love," psychologist Maria P. P. Root explores the topic of interracial marriage. Student reaction papers on the pros and cons of interracial marriage conclude the chapter readings.

Reading 1 (page 208)

An American Success Story Samuel Nakasian

An alternative to the prereading question is to have students brainstorm about their own definition of the American Dream. Summarize the main characteristics on the board. After the reading, students can discuss which aspects of their definition appeared in the reading.

Reflecting on the Reading (page 209)

When discussing question 2, it is important to remember that the audience was a group of people about to become American citizens, which might explain why Nakasian spoke only about the positive aspects of America.

Of the choices available for question 3, b and d are probably the easiest to support with examples from the text. Choice b is closely linked to the many rights and freedoms mentioned in paragraph 3 and also to improvements in society as described in paragraph 8. Choice c is linked to the inscription on the Statue of Liberty mentioned in paragraph 10.

Reading 2 (page 210)

Response to "An American Success Story" *Jowita Drazkowski*

This reading is a response to Nakasian's speech, on page 208.

Reflecting on the Reading (page 212)

For question 1a, the place where the written source is identified is in paragraph 1.
For 1b, effective quotations are found in paragraphs 2 and 5.
For 1c, the first sentence in paragraph 2 and the first sentence in paragraph 3 are effective paraphrases.

For question 2, the problems the writer mentions are the language barrier, racial and ethnic discrimination, and hatred between different groups of people. Question 2 can be developed into a more extended writing assignment if desired.

Question 3 raises the issue of making accurate generalizations. Many students have the tendency to make blanket statements that are inaccurate and in some cases misleading or even offensive. As a follow-up to this question, teachers could bring in samples of generalizations that are overstated and ask students to critique and rewrite them.

Reading 3 (page 212)

America 2050: Immigration and the Hourglass
Alejandro Portes

As a variation on the prereading question, ask students to brainstorm the advantages and disadvantages of immigration to the United States using the following categories: society, economy, culture, and politics. Write the categories on the board and then record the students' responses. After the reading, the class can return to these notes and discuss which points were mentioned in the article.

Reflecting on the Reading (page 216)

Before discussing question 1, refer students to the illustration of the hourglass next to it. Portes uses the image of the hourglass to show that the opportunity to move from the lower paying to higher paying jobs is very small, as symbolized by the narrow center of the hourglass.

In response to question 2, Portes is discussing the positive and negative aspects of the mass media. The media is positive in the sense that a lot of information and entertainment can be made available to a great many people; it is negative in that the media may set up unrealistic expectations for immigrants, who often find that the lifestyle portrayed in the media is far out of reach.

For question 3, most students choose letter c as the best answer.

In response to question 4, you can expect students to have difficulty discerning the differences between group and individual characteristics. A simple test to determine whether a characteristic should be considered group-oriented or individualistic is to ask, "Is this something you can choose or change?" For example, skin pigmentation is not a choice; however, you can choose or change your college major. Some characteristics can cut across both categories, such as social class, which one does not choose at birth but which can be influenced during adult life.

Reading 4 (page 217)

Identity *Shanan Marie Lynch*

When students think about identity, they generally think about it in terms of individual characteristics, such as aspects of their personalities, interests, and relationships. Many students do not generally think of their identities in terms of race, ethnicity, or other group characteristics. In order to bring out both group and individual aspects, ask the following questions: *What aspects of your identity can be described only by people who know you well? What aspects of your identity can be described by people who don't know you well?*

Reflecting on the Reading (page 220)

As a variation on question 1, students can categorize aspects of the writer's identity under the following headings: race, nationality, language, religion, and personal aspects.

Here are examples of possible answers to question 2.

a The relationship between the writer and her grandfather was important in developing her first sense of identity.

b In elementary school, the writer began to distance herself from black and Hispanic children.

c In her teenage years, the writer experienced the rejection of black and Hispanic groups as she tried to fit into each of them.

d As an adult, the writer seems to find acceptance in her church, where there are people of many different backgrounds.

For question 3, here are two examples of sentences that explain the main idea: "You have to create your own identity." "Don't worry about what other people think; be yourself." After students have written their sentences, have them choose one word from the sentence to summarize it. For example, a one-word summary of the first example sentence could be either *identity* or *create*. The summary word can then be said aloud and explained to the class. By reducing the summary to a single word and then explaining that word, students have to consider more carefully the essential concept or message of the essay. As a follow-up, students can do research on the kinds of injustice the writer experienced by typing the keywords *unfair treatment and race* or *unfair treatment in schools* into any major search engine.

Reading 5 (page 220)

The Color of Love *Maria P. P. Root*

To help facilitate the prereading exercise, write the two categories on the board: *Advantages of Intermarriage* and *Disadvantages of Intermarriage*. Record the students' thoughts on each category. After reading the article, the class can return to these notes to determine which aspects were discussed.

Reflecting on the Reading (page 224)

For question 1, either a or b can be supported in the essay. Statement c is not supported because the author explains that couples who intermarry often face a great deal of opposition from within their own families. Statement d is not supported because the author sees intermarriage as one possible solution to America's race problems, but not the only one.

For question 2, some examples of other types of supporting evidence are the use of statistics from the Gallup poll (Par. 3) and the NORC poll (Par. 4), quotes from the writer's interviews (Pars. 13 and 14), and a detailed example of the attitudes toward interracial marriage of South Asian immigrants. As a variation on question 2, ask students to reread the article and identify which supporting statements contain facts and which contain opinions. They can then discuss the value of including both facts and opinions in their own writing.

For question 4, some students may be reluctant to share information about their family situations. If that is the case, students might be asked to describe another family they know.

Reading 6 (page 225)

Color or Real Love? *Yanqin Lan*

This essay was written as a response to "The Color of Love," on page 220.

Reflecting on the Reading (page 228)

For question 1, the author uses the problem of racism in her introduction as the hook to engage the reader. She then introduces the concept of interracial marriage, citing some statistics from the article by Root. She ends the paragraph with some thought-provoking questions on interracial marriage.

For question 2, some of the disadvantages Lan points out are misunderstandings due to different languages (Par. 3), families not accepting the relationship (Par. 4), and the potential loss of cultural identity (Par. 4). Some of the advantages mentioned are the opportunity for the husband and wife to learn about other cultures (Par. 5), the opportunity for the children of mixed marriages to learn about two cultures and sometimes to speak two languages (Par. 5), and the opportunity "to learn how to communicate with other races," which might help solve the problems of racism in our society (Par. 5).

For question 3, an example of a direct quote from the author's mother is in paragraph 7, and an example of an indirect quote from the author's father is in the same paragraph.

Reading 7 (page 228)

Interracial Marriages *Igor Faynzilbert*

This essay was written as a response to "The Color of Love," on page 220.

Reflecting on the Reading (page 231)

For question 1, the thesis statement is the first sentence in paragraph 2.

In response to question 2, the author cites the case of a couple he knows as an example of a successful interracial relationship (Par. 4).

For question 3, the author uses statistics in paragraph 12 to explain why Jews might be more tolerant than other groups regarding interracial marriages.

As an alternative to question 4, students might view one of the commercially available videotapes or DVDs that deal with the issue of interracial marriage. They could then either freewrite in their journals about its relevance to the reading or discuss its relevance in class. Examples of films dealing with interracial marriage are *Guess Who's Coming to Dinner* (1967), *Mississippi Masala* (1991), *Snow Falling on Cedars* (1999), *Monster's Ball* (2001), and *Guess Who* (2005). Note: It is best to view a film before assigning it to make sure the content is suitable for your students.

TECHNIQUES WRITERS USE (pages 231–239)

To prepare for writing a brief research paper, students learn how to support ideas with evidence, paraphrase and quote from sources, and provide proper citation.

Supporting Ideas with Evidence (page 231)

It is important for students to understand that in order for their ideas and opinions to be taken seriously, they must be supported with evidence such as statistics, interviews, observation, or other examples. As a way of introducing this subject, ask the students to brainstorm or freewrite for a few minutes on the question *Why is evidence such as statistics or other data used in a research paper?* As students come up with answers, write them on the board and discuss them as a class.

Task 7.1 *Analyze* (page 232)

The purpose of this task is to raise students' awareness of the different types of evidence a writer can use to support a thesis.

For question 1a, there is an extended quote in paragraph 13.
For 1b, there is a paraphrase at the beginning of paragraph 5.
For question 1c, there are statistics from the Gallup and NORC polls in paragraphs 3 and 4.
For question 1d, there is an extended discussion of how South Asian families regard interracial marriage in paragraph 9.

Task 7.2 *Practice* (page 232)

As a follow-up to this task, students can be asked to do library or online research to locate some of the types of evidence discussed. (Note that one of the options for this chapter's *Essay Assignment* is to write about interracial marriage. Students who chose this option will do online research about intermarriage in the *Internet Search* activity on page 239.)

Paraphrasing and Quoting to Add Support (page 232)

The tasks in this section are designed to allow students to practice the skills of paraphrasing and quoting that are so essential to academic writing.

Task 7.3 *Analyze* (page 233)

For question 1, Lan uses the words "Maria P. P. Root explains this in the article 'The Color of Love'. . ." (Par.1). In paragraph 4, she uses phrases such as "Root explains" or "Root states" to introduce quotes.

There are several examples of paraphrasing of the Root article in paragraph 4 and of the McBride book in paragraph 6.

Task 7.4 *Practice* (page 233)

In this task, students practice paraphrasing and quoting material from a published article. It is important that you allow sufficient time to complete step 6, in which examples of the students' work are discussed with the class.

Giving Credit to Sources (page 234)

In this section, there are examples of MLA and APA styles for citing the types of research materials students most commonly use: books, magazine articles, journal articles, and the Internet. Most humanities professors prefer the MLA style, whereas social scientists tend to use APA. For more detailed information on these styles, consult the latest editions of the *Modern Language Association Style Guide* and the *Publication Manual of the American Psychological Association* or the Web sites for those organizations.

Remind students at this point that even if they paraphrase information from a published or online source, it must be properly cited. In addition to crediting authorship, citations are valuable for those who will read the paper and might want to check the sources themselves. Remind students of the importance of avoiding plagiarism and help them learn what does and doesn't constitute cheating. There are numerous guides available online that can be found by entering the keywords *What is plagiarism?* in the search box of any major search engine.

Task 7.5 *Analyze* (page 238)

For question 1, "Color or Real Love?" uses MLA style; "Interracial Marriages" uses APA.

The following chart illustrates some possible answers for question 2. Please note that this activity is not designed to be a comprehensive analysis of APA or MLA styles but merely points out some common differences between them. Students may refer to examples of MLA and APA styles on pages 235–237.

APA	MLA
In-text reference	
• Comma between name of author and year of publication	• No comma between name of author and year of publication
• If author's name is not in text, work is cited by author's name, year of publication, and page number	• If author's name is not in text, work is cited by author's name and page number
• If author's name is in text, work is cited by year of publication only	• If author's name is in text, work is cited by page number only
• Internet sources with author are cited by author's last name and year of retrieval in parentheses	• Internet sources with author are cited only by author's last name in parentheses

APA	MLA
Bibliography	
References	Works Cited
• Initials of author's first and middle names given	• Full first name of author given; middle initial given
• Works cited by author's last name followed by comma and first initial	• Works cited by author's last name followed by comma, full first name, and middle initial
• Author's name followed by year of book publication or date of article in parentheses	• Author's name followed by title of book or article
• Book titles are italicized	• Book titles are underlined
• Article titles are not italicized	• Article titles are set off by quotation marks
• Article titles in scholarly journals are followed by name of publication, volume number, and then page number(s)	• Article titles in scholarly journals are followed by name of publication, volume number, year of publication, and then page number(s)
• Page numbers of articles are set off by a comma	• Page numbers of articles are set off by a colon

Task 7.6 *Practice* (page 238)

In this task, students practice developing a bibliography. Although the task can be done in either MLA or APA style, choose one style to avoid confusion. See the *Answer Key* on page 262 of the Student's Book.

INTERNET SEARCH (pages 239–240)

The Internet assignments in Option 1 and Option 2 are directly linked to the essay assignments on pages 240–241. (See A *Word of Caution About the Internet* on page 28 of this manual.)

ESSAY ASSIGNMENT (pages 240–245)

In this section guidelines for *Generating Ideas, Organizing Ideas,* and *Working Toward a Thesis Statement* are provided for each of the two essay options.

The use of the Internet has been emphasized throughout the book, but students should also be made aware of the importance of using the library. Despite the tremendous growth of availability of online sources, the vast majority of books and periodicals are not yet available except in actual libraries. The reference librarian in your library should be able to help students find both print and online sources.

Writing Tips (page 245)

The tips in this section are specifically intended for writers working on a research paper.

Writing Your First Draft (page 245)

By this stage of the course, all students should be familiar with the process of drafting, revising, and editing. If necessary, review with students the information in *Writing Your First Draft* on page 14 of this manual.

REVISING YOUR ESSAY (pages 245–246)

By this stage of the course, all students should be familiar with the revising process. If necessary, see *An Overview of the Writing Process* on page 15 of this manual.

When Does Revising End? A Word on Meeting Deadlines (pages 245–246)

Although it is often difficult to get students used to revising, once they are used to it and see its benefits, they may feel reluctant to stop revising and – finally – hand in their writing. This is a good opportunity to let them know that professional writers often feel the same way and that, as Donald Murray says, "A piece of writing is never finished. It is delivered to a deadline . . ."

Writing Your Second Draft (page 246)

Make sure that students fill out the *Writer's Plan for Revising* form before beginning their second drafts. Remind them that although they should seriously consider the feedback they have received from their peers, they must decide for themselves which peer comments are useful and which are not.

EDITING YOUR ESSAY (pages 246–248)

By this stage of the course, all students should be familiar with the editing process. If necessary, see *An Overview of the Writing Process* on page 15 of this manual.

Grammar in Context: Using the Active and Passive Voice of Verbs (page 246)

Some writing teachers tell students to avoid the passive voice as much as possible, and generally this is good advice. However, there are situations when the passive voice is preferable or even necessary. Here are two examples:

"Penicillin was discovered in 1928 but not put in use until the 1940s." In this case, the focus is not on who discovered penicillin but rather when it was discovered and first used.

"The crime rate has been greatly reduced due to a number of new initiatives by the police department." In this case, the emphasis is on the results of the new initiatives rather than on who developed and implemented them.

Task 7.7 **Analyze** (page 247)

See the *Answer Key* on page 262 of the Student's Book.

Task 7.8 **Practice** (page 248)

See the *Answer Key* on page 262 of the Student's Book.

Editing Checklist (page 248)

If necessary, review *What Is Proofreading?* on page 55 of the Student's Book with students before they complete the checklist. Stress the value of proofreading three separate times, each time with a different objective.

A NOTE AS YOU COMPLETE THE COURSE (page 249)

Prior to completing *Assessing Your Progress: A Closing Survey*, on page 254, students should be asked to review the goals they set for themselves in *A Beginning Survey* (page 24), as well as their comments on *A Midterm Survey* (page 122). Allow time to have student-teacher conferences to discuss the closing surveys. These assessment forms are not only beneficial for the student in measuring his or her own progress but also help the teacher in getting feedback on the course.

PARTING WORDS FROM THE AUTHORS (page 249)

In addition to hearing from students, we are always interested in hearing from teachers who have used this book. Comments we received from teachers who used earlier versions of *In Our Own Words* were extremely helpful as we worked on this edition. In addition, we are always on the lookout for good quality student writing for use in future editions of this book or in other books. We hope that you will encourage your students to send us their writing either by e-mailing us directly or giving it to you to e-mail to us. We look forward to hearing from you and your students and wish you much success.

Please send any correspondence or essays to us electronically at:
Rebecca Mlynarczyk, <rmlynarczyk@kbcc.cuny.edu>
Steven Haber, <shaber@njcu.edu>